PEACHES KAWAMATA

Naked in the Dining Room

Copyright © 2024 by Peaches Kawamata

All rights reserved. No part of this publication may be reproduced, stored or transmitted in any form or by any means, electronic, mechanical, photocopying, recording, scanning, or otherwise without written permission from the publisher. It is illegal to copy this book, post it to a website, or distribute it by any other means without permission.

Peaches Kawamata has no responsibility for the persistence or accuracy of URLs for external or third-party Internet Websites referred to in this publication and does not guarantee that any content on such Websites is, or will remain, accurate or appropriate.

While every precaution has been taken in the preparation of this book, the publisher assumes no responsibility for errors or omissions, or for damages resulting from the use of the information contained herein.

Second edition

This book was professionally typeset on Reedsy.
Find out more at reedsy.com

Contents

Foreword

My dirty secret isn't that I was a stripper. I'm proud of being a stripper. My dirty secret is that I was a terrible waitress for so damn long.

I have worked in food service for twenty-seven years. I started as a teenage dishwasher. I've been a busser, a runner, a host, a waiter, a bartender, a manager, a beverage director. I've worked food prep and expo and as a buffet attendant and as a menu designer. I've worked fine dining, casual, upscale casual, and at summer camps.

And for most of my time in the industry, I was terrible at dealing with customers. I felt angry, I felt put-upon, I felt like "the help." Every special request and difficult guest exhausted me. It wasn't until I began to think of restaurant work as sex work that everything became easier, more profitable, and honestly: fun.

My tenure as a stripper was much shorter than I had planned. When the pandemic hit in 2020 I just never felt safe going back. While I was there, it was my absolute dream job. About once a day I had to pinch myself (of course, I charged myself for the pleasure). I was so thrilled to walk around feeling like a goddess. I couldn't believe I had a stage all to myself several times a night for naked interpretive dance to my favorite music – 80's hair metal, if you're asking. I loved being desired and I loved being able to monetize men's desire. I loved doting on my appearance with makeup, moisturizer, and manicures in a way the outside world would find excessive and vain. In the club, it is just part of the job.

Most of all, I loved being around all these powerful women and feeling powerful myself. The power of strippers absolutely took my breath away. These are women who stare down the the most razing accusations our society can level at women: WHORE, DUMB, VAIN, GREEDY, SELFISH, DUPLICITOUS, FAKE and walk directly into them, walk around proudly in them, and make their living in them. They wouldn't even bat an eye at being called "the help."

In the outside world, men run the show. Women are ignored and disrespected in business. We are paid less for the same labor. Crimes committed against our physical selves aren't investigated, let alone solved. We fawn and flutter around eligible male partners and worry if they like us, if they love us. We are taught to long for marriage, when marriage statistically benefits men to a staggering degree. We manage the household, the children, the schedule, and are hated as nags. If we embrace femininity and sexuality, we are laughed off as cheap women. If we step outside of performative femininity, we are derided as dykes and manhaters.

There is simply no choice I can make and the world will reward me. The best I can hope for is to be permitted to exist as a lesser citizen. So why would I concern myself with the cultural mores of a society stacked against me?

I don't. I cannot force the world to value me. What I can do is slip down between the cracks in society to the places the world doesn't want to admit exist. I can ignore the insults on the way down. And I can thrive there.

"Selling your body" is a phrase used to deride sex work. But we all sell our bodies in our labor. The coal miner risks the safety of his body, the function of his lungs, and the time his body spends away from the sunlight. All of that in exchange for wages. A database administrator stares at a computer all day, his body engaged in one of the most dangerous activities possible: sitting. Cooks are burned. Servers' backs and knees hurt from walking endless miles on concrete floors. Everyone's body is for sale.

What's really frowned upon is a woman selling my attractiveness, my nakedness, my sex appeal, and selling the idea that I have a more intimate connection with a man than I do. I've never felt more taken advantage of than in straight jobs, office jobs. In an office job, I still have to put up with everything I do from men in the club, but for free. It is terrifying to the world that a woman could have the power to market what I am expected to do for nothing.

In the strip club, women don't need to beg for approval. The second a man steps foot into the club, he has signaled his weakness. His need. If he could get what he was looking for without paying for it, he would have driven there, not parked his car at the club.

We know they need us when they're in the club.

All the skills we were forced to hone in the outside world for survival suddenly become our ticket to a man's wallet. And all the skills the world rewards him for are rendered absolutely useless. We learned to fawn, to make him feel smart, to de-escalate his anger, to salve his insecurities. He learned women owe him their time, their kindness, their patience, and their bodies. In the club they owe him nothing. In the club, he pays for those things.

These skills are naturally transferable to front of house work, and this book will show you how. These are techniques that will make hosts, servers, bartenders, and bar managers fabulously good at their jobs, and will elevate that restaurant from banal to elite. If you've lived as a woman or been powerless for any length of time in your life, you probably already instinctively know how.

But it isn't pretty. These techniques are acquired and perfected in moments of survival. They exemplify everything society tells us we shouldn't be. To successfully utilize them, we surrender any hope of the approval from society at large, and the illusion of safety it offers. To embody them, we threaten our sense of self. If you are willing to step through that doorway, then you can access tools very few possess.

Host

"Lakes and rivers are lords of the hundred valleys. Why? Because they'll go lower. So they're the lords of the hundred valleys. Just so, a wise soul, wanting to be above other people, talks to them from below and to guide them, follows them."

- Tao Te Ching by Lao Tzu (Translated by Ursula K. LeGuin)

—

The most frightening moment of your restaurant experience is when you step through the door. This is the moment you give up control of your experience and hope someone else can fulfill your dreams. Opening the door and stepping into that mood lighting is like jumping off a cliff and hoping someone catches you.

The host catches you. The host makes sure that terrifying moment ends in beautiful relief. You can only relinquish control if you believe you will be taken care of. The host must instill trust that every decision being made for you is for your benefit.

It is imperative that the first moment of terror ends as soon as possible. Ideally, you will walk in and see a bright face exuding joy at your arrival. If the host is on the phone, just a smile and a wave can be enough to staunch the terror. If the host is away from the door, the rest of the staff knows to immediately greet you and let you know you won't be waiting long. Whether you're a regular or brand new to this restaurant, that moment of connection is imperative.

Walking into a club is terrifyingly intimidating. Walking into a club, a man is admitting he needs sexual stimulation and emotional connection.

When he walks into a club, the presence of big unsmiling men imply he had better be on his best behavior. It's dark (really dark) except for the seizure-inducing light show that intermittently blinds him. He is standing in front of a beautiful (yet clothed) woman elevated behind a desk where he pays for entry. Even she has a tip bowl – we teach him immediately nothing is for free and everyone gets a tip. It's loud, even during the day. As he rounds the corner, he sees half naked goddesses in tiny dresses strolling around, towering over him in glittery high heels you don't see on regular women. The room opens up to a stage that rises high above the floor with a pole in the middle. A girl in a pink thong and clear heels hangs upside down lazily from the pole by her strong thighs, the nipple rings in her naked tits glinting in the swooping spotlights that slash across the stage. There are cozy little seats and tiny tables all over the room that look like good spots for cocktails and intimate conversations. There are gorgeous couches and little alcoves partitioned off that say "VIP ONLY," and he stays far away from those, knowing he most certainly is not a VIP and doesn't want to be confused with one. He glances around, titillated, but terrified. He is excited to be here but overwhelmed with uncertainty of how to behave. And then, a smiling, friendly goddess with a happy, open face walks toward him like she was waiting for him, and his terror immediately eases.

At the club, there were plenty of regulars who were used to the way things worked, and they had all fallen into their own groove. There was a guy who loved to talk about how he had once dated a stripper who worked there (she was long gone) and truly thought himself our friend. He had bleached hair, stainless steel jewelry, and full sleeves of tattoos. He never bought a dance, but I always made sure to say "hi" to him and give him a hug, and he always made sure to tuck $5 in my thong when I was onstage. There was an enormous fellow of about 50, tall and broad, who would never get a dance, but if you sat with him, he'd pay for your drinks as long as you wanted them. He liked to come to the stage and stand a little too close, at an angle the bouncers couldn't see. As I purposely let my naked body graze his gray polo shirt, he would tell me a dirty joke and give me a dollar. There was a tiny round man who barely spoke any English, but would pick a girl and take her for an hour private room in the middle of lunch. My least favorite guy came almost every day just to get lunch on his break from work and never spend a dime on the dancers. He just loved that chicken cheesesteak and free tits onstage too much to quit. (I still have dreams of passing behind him as he stuffed his face and "accidentally" smearing his collar with a fuckload of pink glitter to explain to his wife later.)

Spotting a man with a slightly dazed look walking slowly as his eyes adjust to the darkness was a huge opportunity for me. He doesn't even know what kind of customer he wants to be. It is up to me to tell him.

I ask his name right away. I say it early, I never forget it, I roll it over in my mouth like it is a delicious candy. I look him deep in his eyes when I say it. There is no sound anyone likes more than their own name. There is no greater hurt than having their name forgotten. No one can help the release of happy chemicals when they hear it.

Strippers don't use their real names because of very real safety issues. We don't want to be stalked or followed or found outside the club. But it is important to make men think it is a real name. If I use something clearly theatrical like "Peaches" it is important to have a secret second fake name. I would be very reluctant to tell a man my second fake name, but finally I would say something like, "I think I can trust you. Peaches is just my stage name. My real name is Elizabeth." He feels closer to me, knowing my "real" name, and that will make it easier to build a relationship.

In restaurants, our guests' names are written down for us, right in the reservation book. We have free access to the sound you like most in the world. And when you tell us your name tentatively, your voice hovering in a question, suddenly deeply anxious that for some reason your reservation doesn't exist, and therefore perhaps YOU don't exist, as host, I have a great opportunity. I can appear as excited to say your name as you are to hear it. You just brushed against existential dread, and I can relieve that. I can affirm your personhood.

In the club, with my little newborn fawn of a man, I act like his friend. Many first timers are guys unfamiliar and uncomfortable with the concept of exchange of money for intimacy, and they need to feel safe enough to work up to it. I take on a girl-next-door energy. Attainable. Kind. Familiar. I tell them (without revealing too much, of course) about how the club works. I tell them harmless little details about the other dancers (usually made up) as we watch them onstage. I would even encourage and accompany them to sit near the stage and tip a dancer to get them used to spending money. My foolproof tactic was to take them on a tour. "Those booths are where I do lap dances. There is the bar. There is another bar upstairs, can I show you?"

Once I've gotten him to his feet it's all over. By the time we end at the private rooms upstairs, he felt I had given him so much for free: a tour, all those tickly feelings of saying his name, and being his guide to this scary environment, that he thinks he owes me. So he is excited to take me for a private room.

Giving someone something freely, before they ask for it, creates a psychological sense of debt. And the easiest thing to give away for free is flattery. There is a moment of delicious relief when you learn that your reservation exists and you, by extension, also exist, that you will NOT be left alone in the restaurant to fend for yourself. In this moment, a compliment will almost certainly overload your brain with pleasure. It will also set up a power dynamic where you feel you owe the host something, and you become slightly more open to influence.

In the club, I always directed my compliments to men based on two things: their physical appearance and their uniqueness among other men. Everyone in the world to some degree will wonder, when they aren't getting enough sexual attention: is it because of my appearance? By complimenting them on their appearance specifically, I can help obscure the transactional nature of our interaction. "You're so hot, I bet you get lots of ladies… I love your eyes… I always end up dating short kings like you… (Yeah, you're TECHNICALLY paying me money for a dance, but I'm into it because of how hot you are.)"

Men don't want to think they HAVE to pay for attention from beautiful women. But they are happy to, if they feel like they have a shot. Every civilian man I've ever talked to, when I tell them I've been a stripper, immediately tells me a story about that one time they went to a club and a stripper was super into them. I always laugh to myself, not because these men got played, but because they got exactly what they needed. I laugh with amazement that strippers the world over know the product they are selling isn't a dance. We are selling the hope of a sparkling relationship with a sexy woman.

"Being taken advantage of" is a sore idea some men harbor in deep insecurity. There is so much talk about "you're just after my money." They are used to getting at least a laugh for free from women, and usually much more. They bristle at the very concept of paying for attention.

One time, I was talking to an terrible asshole. In an effort to seem not completely available to him, a product in high demand, I responded to a text in front of him. "Sorry, my friends are blowing me up."

"Customers, you mean," he said. He didn't even see me as a human with a life outside of the club. Just a man-devouring thresher. This man saw the club as highly transactional. He saw the strippers as laborers.

We must uphold the fantasy that we are attainable, because many men feel insulted to have to pay for dances. EVEN THOUGH THEY WALKED INTO A STRIP CLUB. They feel tiny, like one in a long line of men. They desperately want to feel a connection (that's why they came) and are desperate for us to prove to them this ISN'T transactional. The experience of the dance, a gorgeous lady in your lap, her smelling great, giving him all her attention, that is not enough. The experience must be unique to him to reflect his unique importance in the world.

I use compliments to reinforce their uniqueness. "Guys like you don't really come in here! This is a real treat for me!" They feel special, then, which is exactly the secret desire we all have. "I'm worthy, I'm special, just by being me, and someday someone wonderful will reinforce this."

In a restaurant, I never compliment physical features. I run the risk of stumbling upon a landmine of hidden insecurity. You aren't coming to restaurants to affirm your worthiness for sexual connection. "You're so pretty!" could be interpreted as "I'm too fat to be complimented on my figure." "I love your hair!" could seem totally generous and innocent, but you could have just gotten a haircut your husband hates and he's being really mean about it.

I only compliment things that you have clearly chosen that day. Accessories are by far the safest. When you decided to go to dinner, you picked your red suede purse on purpose because you like it for a reason meaningful only to you. If I draw attention to that, I give you an immediate dopamine hit. It reinforces that you're on the right track, this you, today, right now. Earrings and eyeglasses are also top notch for compliments, as they are carefully chosen and often fretted over. Rings and necklaces are a little riskier, as they can often be tied to lost loved ones or indicate stressed relationships. A foolproof compliment references the reason for a reservation: "A girls' night out! That is such a lovely idea! I need to do that." All else fails, I compliment reservation times. "Oh my goodness, you made such a good choice eating at 5pm, you are going to catch this gorgeous afternoon sunshine."

And yes, all these examples are compliments for women and femmes. These people appear less often in clubs. And when they do I absolutely SLATHER them in compliments about their appearance. Women compare themselves to strippers, even if they are attracted to us. If a straight couple comes into the club I all but ignore the man and let the woman know how gorgeous and hot and funny and sexy and exciting she is. I love her hair. I love the size of her tits. I love her outfit and where did she get it because I need it.

If I were to give attention to the man, I change the dynamic to that of competition between me and the woman. Useless for my sales purposes, and nothing more the world needs: women are forced to compete enough. I find it thrilling to have an opportunity to bolster a woman's self-esteem. I'm excited that they found their way to the club, to see the power of strippers. I want her to be able to feel that energy here so she can carry it into the world.

Women outside of the club, especially women of a certain age, walk around in terror. The world tells them to have a healthy appetite, but also never to get fat. It tells them to be attractive to men, to be a sexual freak, but also to not fuck whomever they like. They've spent their lives dieting, and putting up with emotionally unavailable husbands, and putting themselves through hell contorting themselves to just be allowed to exist. Do men see this? Can they see the brittleness in civilian women like we can?

They walk into restaurants ready to shatter, primed to be taken apart by the smallest inconvenience, because their entire life has put them on edge. And they are also (understandably) the demographic least capable of relinquishing control. They feel like they are barely holding on even by forcing all their willpower on the world. They barely have what they need now, and if they were to let go, it would all fall apart. They need to feel extra safe in these first few moments with the host.

They are also going to need an extra firm hand to guide their experience and navigate choice overwhelm. After guests are properly greeted, named, and complimented, we must instill confidence that their experience will be amazing and hand-picked for them specifically by their new best friends: us.

No matter your demographic, I tell you, "follow me!" cheerfully, rewarding you for relinquishing control. You don't have to think now. You don't have to lead. You don't have to manage the outcome. Just follow me. Before we even start walking, I tell you something wonderful about your table and why it is perfect for you. "Oh I have the cutest little banquette table for you!" or "This table has so much sunshine, you're going to love it!" or "This is where the owner eats when she's here!"

It can be particularly frightening at this point if you are walking into an empty restaurant. Look at all the choices! Do you trust the host, really, to care for you? Which is the best table in the restaurant? You certainly don't have enough information to pick, nor do you have enough to trust. Even if we've primed you with how great this table is, in a dearth of empty tables, you will blanche. It may not even matter if we take you to the best table, you may ask for another table just to test if you still have control.

To host is to manage an ever changing jigsaw puzzle. There is a lot you don't see about why you are being seated at a particular table. We are managing filling the restaurant all night, evenly seating the servers, closing down one section early, specific table requests, not to mention last minute emergencies. The couple in the corner who are taking three hours to eat when we only budgeted them two. The server crying in the walk-in fridge and can't take tables. The bartender running to the store to buy more ice.

And the honest truth is: there are very few "bad" tables. We absolutely seat you at the best tables first. When the restaurant is already full, you won't even notice if you're at a less-great table. Your brain will only register gratitude that you "snagged" a table. Our most important job as host is to gain your trust in our ability to care for you. To transition you from the person trying to control it all out there, to a person worthy of care in here. So in fact, it is in our best interest to seat you at the best table available so you feel taken care of.

And: so you won't ask to move.

If you do have a last minute panic and ask for a different table, I frame my answer in forced choice. "That table is reserved, but I am happy to seat you at table A or table B." You get to make a choice to feel safe, and I get to manage the flow of the restaurant at large.

The strip club where I worked had lots of different products to buy. A dance on the floor, in front of everyone: bra comes off. That was the cheapest. Lap dances in the semi-private booths for a little more. Private rooms for 15 minutes, 30 minutes, or an hour. Obviously, an hour room (with complimentary champagne) was the most expensive, and made me the most money. Now, there is no menu posted anywhere so men can know this. The club charges dancers for the rooms, but dancers can also set their own prices for their time. The only access men have to this information is me.

I would offer a forced choice early in our conversation. "Should we get a 30 minute room or an hour room?" I have framed in his mind that the choice between those two things is normal and appropriate.

All day long you are inundated with limitless choices. Human brains are not equipped to operate with the number of choices we encounter in modern life. It is exhausting. And with limitless choices comes the limitless guilt. Did you choose correctly? What if you chose something different, would you be happier? It's a pain that thrums constantly in the background. A limited choice is a relief. A limited choice is part of the gift of care that strip clubs and restaurants offer. Here, you don't have to figure it out.

I can see on your faces after I limit your choice of tables that you still feel uneasy, unbalanced, in terror at relinquishing control. I can see men terrified that they agreed to spend hundreds of dollars with no guarantee they are going to get what they hope for. And some guests will never let go. Some men will never be satisfied. But I know that look of unease is not about outcomes. It's about how scary it is to let go.

Of course, forced choice is also a technique to manipulate my desired outcome. I want you to sit where I need you to sit, AND I need to maintain a sense of resource scarcity. You can't have ANY table you want. You're my special new best friend and I would LOVE to give you any table you want, but there are those more elite than you. They are the ones that can have anything they want. Wouldn't it be nice if you could? But you're just lucky to be here. You're lucky to even have gotten a reservation.

While working in a quaint bistro, I once had these regulars that were a complete dream. A white straight couple in their late 50's, they probably fell in love as homecoming king and queen and never were passed over for a promotion. Pure naive, blond

Americana. They were kind, they were thoughtful, and they tipped generously. When they made a reservation, they always requested a certain table which we were happy to hold for them. Soon, they stopped making reservations and still expected their special table. Then, they decided maybe that table wasn't really the best table after all, and could they have that other one? The last time they came to the restaurant, they asked to move twice, to two brand new tables. They were dissatisfied, grumpy, and the manager had to bend over backwards to even get them to finish their meal.

We must maintain a sense that this experience is an elite, elusive, hard to come by resource that we bestow only to the most worthy. If we don't, the veil is drawn and we become simply a product you can buy. A gas station coffee. A drive-through burger. Something of great availability and low value. Even regulars can never become so comfortable that they get exactly what they want all the time. There must always be an illusion that someone is more important than them. No one, not even my most elite VIP, can know that he is my most elite VIP. Our clients must always feel grateful for our service and never entitled to it.

"You can barely get a reservation at that place!" Is the exact buzz we want. Everyone knows what that means: this restaurant is SO GOOD that it is worth it to work for a reservation, to wait months, and (once attained) an item of great value you feel lucky to have and behave appropriately to keep.

Exclusivity means you will be happy to wait (as long as you are greeted appropriately.) In fact, waiting for a table makes you feel like you have entered an elite space. Waiting for a table, even with a reservation, is not only normal in a sought after restaurant, it is beneficial to set the tone of the evening: we are in charge. You can trust us to take care of you, but it will be an experience created by us, not by you. I never apologize for guests waiting for a table, as that will tilt the power back to you.

I communicate clearly: "Your table isn't quite ready, and I think we are looking at about a ten minute wait."

I offer options: "You're welcome to have a drink at the bar or wait in our outdoor area."

But I never apologize. If you think this is an aberration instead of an expectation, you feel like we don't have control of the situation.

I had a regular at the club who was reliable for one dance and a reasonable tip. Basically about as much as could buy me a burger and a beer. He liked to chat for about 15 minutes before the dance. As he got used to this arrangement, the chatting time got longer and longer. He was eating up time I wasn't able to spend giving dances to other men. Several other dancers had abandoned him altogether for this behavior. But even if it was a measly burger and a beer, it was a reliable burger and a beer. I would chat with him for a time frame that felt appropriate to me, and then I would ask him if he was ready for a dance. If he said no, I'd just walk away. I'd say I had to go to the bathroom. Or even just say I was going to try to get a dance from another man. One day he came in and I had no patience at all, so without even sitting down I asked him, "do you want a dance now or later?" and when he said later, I happily said "come get me!" and walked away.

I knew this would work with him specifically for a very weird reason: he wore a girdle. I could feel it when I was giving him a dance, the little train track of eye hooks going up the center of his belly, and the weird tautness under his shirt. He was a round, short guy in his sixties with a mustache, a real Budweiser and beach dude. And in his mind he was absolutely not having transactional experience. He was trying to appear more attractive to me. And when the supply of my time was perceived as more in demand, he immediately began to do what he needed to get it.

He gave me a Christmas present that year, just as cheap as he was: a lump of coal and a $5 Starbucks gift card that I still carry in my wallet. I keep it to remind myself how valuable my time is.

Server

"The polity of greatness runs downhill like a river to the sea, joining with everything, woman to everything. By stillness the woman may always dominate the man, lying quiet underneath him. Lie low to be on top, be on top by lying low."

-Tao Te Ching by Lao Tzu (Translated by Ursula K. LeGuin)

—

The second your butts hit the seats, a new terror arises in your gut. You're out here, uncared for, abandoned, forgotten. Your one ally, the host, is gone, with vague promises that a server will be here shortly. And now you have zero choices. You can't walk away when you're sitting down. You're adrift on your raft of a table, and you don't even have any water.

The second your butts hit the seats, a clock starts. Every second we don't come greet you, your trust in our ability to care for you erodes. We must get those water glasses filled as soon as humanly possible. Even if we are slammed, our priority list shifts down to make our new table our number one. Having someone else fill your water glasses is a good start, but the sooner we can let you know you are not alone, the better. And the sooner we can get your first round drinks to you, the sooner you will be in a nice cozy cocoon of trust.

If the clock ticks too long, if you sit in that fear too long…well, we're fucked. You'll never relax. You'll never relinquish. You'll be primed to search for mistakes. You'll remind us about things you worry we forgot, even if we haven't. You'll flag us down on our way back to you. The most important thing you wanted from your night you didn't get: to be cared for. To step out of your life into a creative space. To be someone a little different, a little better.

Your entire journey so far in the restaurant is the most important and delicate time for us. If we can navigate you through the host and to your first round of drinks without issue and without fuckups, we've got your trust for the rest of the evening. Your entrees may take 40 minutes. We may be sold out of your favorite dessert. And you'll forgive it all. It all depends on successfully transitioning you into trust in these delicate first few interactions.

As a server, I don't have much time to build a personal connection to you. I must be perceived as an ally, and fast. I must stand in a way that tells you you're being cared for. I must telegraph confidence in a way that makes you trust me and feel safe enough to relinquish power to me. Body language is one of the server's most potent tools.

I need you to think that I have all the time in the world for you. As counter-intuitive it is, even if I can sense my section burning to the ground behind me, carnage and terror and destruction, even if I am remembering appetizers I never ordered and bottles of wine I never opened and the chef is trying to track me down to yell at me, my hips and feet must remain pointed directly at your table. This will always save time. If you sense that I'm desperate to go off and do something else, you'll need more time from me in reassurance. If the time I spend at your table is calm, still, and entirely focused on you, I can get away with a lot less of it.

Different restaurant atmospheres have different expectations of formality. An old school steak-and-lobster-tuxedo-shirt-tableside-ceaser-salad joint will require a little more starch in my posture, a little more showy ceremony in my movements. In this kind of restaurant, I'm playing the invisible help. I'm the butler. I'm making things appear and disappear quietly so you can play the role of aristocrat, or oligarch, or sugar daddy. I take on a symmetrical stance, not shifting my weight into either hip. I clasp my hands behind me or in front of me to indicate I have complete control over my body, and therefore complete control over guiding your experience. I use a quick nod to indicate absorption of command. You don't need my approval, my friendship, or my input. You need me to make you feel you have more power in here than you have out in the world.

Upscale casual (and even some fine dining) requires an illusion of my friendship. As you talk, I am slowly leaning closer and closer to you, as if I'm hanging on your every word. And when you reach the punchline, I send my whole body backward again in laughter. You've so deeply moved me, you've moved my whole body. If I am writing in a notebook, I am also covering my soft underside from predators. I purposefully make sure to lower the notebook when I can, making the reveal of my belly even more of a gift of vulnerability to you, my friend, someone I trust deeply and whom would never eviscerate me.

I avoid initiating physical contact. I have no idea how you will feel about it. I casually put my arm around the backs of chairs to mime putting my arm around your shoulders. You may be touch averse due to trauma or as a general preference. You may read it as a controlling act, and I need you to believe I am utterly available to your whims. You may read it as a legitimate sexual advance, and whether that is welcome or unwelcome, not a door necessary to unlock as your server.

In the club, just walking around, maintaining a sense of "not quite having control over my body" is really important. Dress straps that constantly fall down are great. Being so at ease it looks like I'm in my own living room. Touching men's arms like I don't even notice I just touched a stranger. It's not just that men are attracted to confidence in a woman (some are not), it is that men are looking for a stripper that's willing to blur the lines of a transactional experience. Whether they want full-service sex work like blow jobs or fucking in the club (which we called "extras") or they want me to be their girlfriend outside of the club, they need an indication that I am a little wild. A little out of control. A little fine with breaking the rules. The rules which prevent them from getting what they actually want: a sincere personal connection.

Costuming is a desperately important part of my repertoire. In a club, there is only one thing I'm trying to evoke with my costume: SEX. I want to look like a viable, vibrant, sexual partner. I want you to picture yourself fucking me. It is upon that image I build my entire career.

And it needs to be simple. We are painfully aware that men want us to be very easy to digest. If they can't process something about my costume, if they can't place it within their preconceived notion of "perfect ideal," their brains glitch and they move on to another stripper. Even an unusually dark lipstick shade or asymmetrical dress can be enough to overwhelm a man's circuits. Real women are complicated and multifaceted. Men will pay for the illusion that women are simple.

Costuming is no less important in restaurants, and more subtle. We are trying to gain your trust in a different arena than viable sexual partnership. Through costuming, we are telegraphing that you won't be left alone, and that your needs will be met. Any costume that can include obvious attention to detail is valuable. A tie neatly tied. Perfect color coordination. Blacks that match (and don't appear gray or blue). Hairstyles that appear purposeful and stay in place. Obviously, anything dirty or wrinkled will only erode your trust that we can attend to details. If we can't even notice something on our own person, how will we anticipate your needs?

And we don't discount utilizing our sexuality. For women or femme servers, wearing tight or low cut costumes still works well. There is one instance when they don't: if a heterosexual woman guest perceives you as a threat. We have so little control over this scenario, however. We could be totally professional and formal, and just showing off our boobs a little may be enough for cold and judgmental looks. We could shower her with all the attention and ignore her date, and it still may not be enough. Usually, though, we don't need her approval if the man is paying. A nice tip from her husband is worth more than any cold and judgmental look.

We telegraph a lot through our body language and our costuming the character we think you will like, but the single greatest skill for a stripper or server is to be able to intuit who you want us to be.

Do you stop talking and turn your entire body towards me as I approach the table? Then you probably want me to be a strong guide to your experience. You crave my approval for being a good customer.

Do you crack a joke as soon as you can? Then you want me to be a good audience member, or perhaps a sparring partner.

Do you actively ignore me? Then you want a subservient attendant to make you feel powerful.

We happily slip into each role.

I started stripping at 38. It had been a dream of mine, I realize now, for my entire life. It was something so hidden in me I couldn't even admit it to myself. When I left a short, unhappy marriage at 37, I felt old expectations for my life crumbling. And when my mind first identified the desire to be a stripper, my stomach started to hurt. It was such a real and pure desire, it was almost too much to consider. And like staring directly into the sun: painful. My age, my inexperience, the lack of resources, it seemed like too much. It was certainly too late. I put it out of my mind. And then my stomach would start hurting again.

Luckily, becoming a stripper isn't as hard as becoming an astronaut. I just danced around with my tits out for some slimy manager. He thought I was hot. I was hired. I don't have many regrets in life, but not stripping sooner is the biggest.

It's common for restaurant employees to wax poetic about how everyone should work in a restaurant for a year. About all the valuable skills you learn there and nowhere else: patience, humility, kindness, problem-solving. Working a physical job in a frantic environment. The smart, hopeful, clever young women I work with in restaurants, I wish I could tell them: try stripping. All young women should strip for a year. The power I accessed inside myself, the strength, the pride, the comfort in my body, the absolute inability to put up with the bullshit of men: it was unparalleled to everything I'd learned up until I was 38. I wish I'd learned it all sooner.

But when you're a stripper at 38, men don't want to know you're 38. I usually told them I was 27 (hey, it's dark in there.) One long-time regular pointed out another stripper, a gorgeous and successful lady, and said, "you see her? She's like FORTY and she's been here FOREVER!" I put on my most amazed and innocent face and said "Wow!"

On my first day, a man in his mid-twenties asked me, "How

old are you? You seem really young." I immediately started slouching a little more, let my shoulders draw down, and started to drop my chin. I made myself look less confident. I let my voice start to go higher. In no conceivable universe did I look 23, but this guy was absolutely telling me who he wanted me to be "really young." So, I told him I was 23.

And he was surprised. "Oh, that's not so young." I learned later that this guy likes to get the new girls in a private room and test their boundaries, so he wants them to be young. He HOPES they are young so that he has more chance of getting girls to do something they don't want to.

He took me to a private room. But he walked out halfway through the dance when it became clear I wouldn't be giving him a handjob. I kept the money.

I knew a new stripper who called herself "Antonia." She was 18 and super nervous. She chatted nonstop, telling me all about her life. She was terrified of going onstage for the first time. It was a privilege to watch her come into her confidence. She became bold, strong, and even quite good at the pole. She could hold her own against any man that came into the club. Antonia was a light-skinned black girl with gorgeous curls. She told me she regretted choosing her name because she didn't realize that men would immediately mistake her for being Latina. It happened over and over, and in her exhaustion she finally started leaning into it. She told me that she had sat down with one man who immediately asked her, "What's Mexico like?"

Without hesitation she replied: "hot!"

The important thing is that I don't internalize my role. I don't get offended if you don't want to talk to me. I don't find it demeaning to laugh at your stupid jokes while your family rolls their eyes. I don't need to correct a man that I'm 38 and not 18, if he wants to take an 18 year old for a private dance (even if that is absolutely bonkers– it's not THAT dark in the club.) Antonia didn't lose any of her identity by not explaining her exact cultural heritage to the men that wanted to pay her to bounce in their laps.

Server is my favorite position in the restaurant, and I think the one most akin to stripping. The server must release the need to be known in order to better know you. The server must change themselves with mercurial ease to be who you want. The server must slide easily into the cracks that you need filling.

Holding tight to the need to be known, to have a solid, mono-lithic sense of self only makes you vulnerable. It's like handing out a pamphlet on your strengths and weaknesses. As a guest, you long to be known. You long to be seen. You long for the reinforcement that you, this self, is worthy.

As a server, I understand this is not a reciprocal relationship. Even if you're kind, even if I wait on you many times over the years, you are here to be known. And I am here to know you. I put my own needs to be known somewhere else in the world, in some other relationship.

And yet, this is not a loss of self. This is not a subservient position. This is a superpower. We aren't serving you. We're creating your experience precisely within our plan. You're not in control. We are.

Creating your experience is not like directing a play. And with all this talk of costumes and roles and body movement you could not be faulted that thinking stripping or working front of house is akin to acting. It is not. Acting is an art; this is not.

Everyone agrees that actors are acting. We may be moved by a performance, we may even be deeply attached to a character. The important part is that we understand it is fiction.

When we're stripping, when we're working in restaurants, only we know we are acting. You think you're interacting with an entirely authentic human. There are no intimacy coordinators, no directors, no bodyguards. We create a beautiful illusion, and however that takes hold inside your head is out of our control. That's so dangerous. You hear about actors getting lost inside a role, getting damaged by it. But they can work to untangle that with the knowledge that the character lives only in the safe world of the theater or the studio.

In the club everyone treats dancers like garbage except us. The owners make it clear that we're easily replaceable cogs in a machine. We aren't even employees; we're contractors. The men who come to the club say the cruelest shit right to our faces. They can barely contain their rage at having to spend money on us. The other dancers are direct competition. Everyone resents the money we make. We grease the gears by tipping everyone, every shift: the bartender, the DJ, the bouncers. Even "Mom" (the strippers' female manager) tries to sell us shit in the dressing room: purses, heels, and dresses. No one thinks we earn our money and everyone wants a piece of it. Everyone works really hard to let us know how worthless and replaceable we are, despite being the main attraction.

Our sense of self is so blurry in this work. You think it's all real, and sometimes we forget it's not. When a man doesn't want a dance from us, it is so easy to internalize that. Are we ugly? Disgusting? When the world calls strippers stupid, slutty, damaged women, could that be true about me? If a guest is cruel in a restaurant, are they being cruel to a fictional character or do I personally deserve it? And what if we try to engage in relationships with clients outside the club or restaurant? That can be physically dangerous for us.

There is no shortage of stories of strippers being murdered by clients. Of clients stalking us or assaulting us outside the club. I used a rideshare service to get to and from work. Benefits were: not having my own car to be followed or recognized by a client at home. Costs were: driving everyday with a stranger who could develop his own fixation. I always dressed really shabbily and changed inside the club, and changed again before I left. I never had the driver pick me up in front of my house, and I had him drop me off at a hotel within walking distance of my home.

Aside from all the practical work I personally put into rideshare spy shit, it takes such intense emotional work to keep up our sense of self-worth.

That's not art. That's so, so much harder.

In art, in a movie or TV show, if there is an intimate scene, the actors and the directors talk through issues of consent and approach the scene in a way that everyone can feel safe with physical touch. However, the biggest misrepresentation of strip clubs in TV and movies is that we don't get touched by men. Nobody takes us for a private dance and says, "I just want to watch."

We get touched all the time. They even touch us when we're onstage, right in front of the bouncers. If I decided I wanted to, men would absolutely have sex with me every day in the club. They think that's what happens there. We're always on defense. And our defense has to be in away that STILL makes them think we'd fuck them right here if it weren't for "the rules." I remember watching a particularly oily dude eat an entire filet of salmon and french fries, push the bites of salmon onto his fork with his fingers, lick them, wipe his hands on his jeans and then take me to a private room.

The very first man I approached on my very first day touched me on the arm as we were chatting. I ripped it away. There was a heavy moment of quiet between us as we both understood what a terrible mistake I had made. He knew I wasn't into him; I knew I could never prove I was. The hardest and most important skill I learned as a stripper was to not recoil in disgust when a stranger touched me. To lean in instead of backing away. To open my arms instead of crossing them over my vulnerable belly. And that skill has translated excellently to the restaurant.

It's so much more powerful in a restaurant, even. There is no expectation that touching the server is appropriate. I would be well within my rights if I were to rip my arm away when an azalea-faced white-guy grampa in a polo shirt strokes my tattoos. I could tell him to go fuck himself. I could get another server to take the table. No one in the service industry should be touched without their permission. But no one in the sex industry should, either.

Except I know that if they touch me: that's good. I get a thrill of power surge through me. I can control my reactions to them, but they are helpless in their reactions to me. They can't help but reach out and touch me. They are stupidly telling me that they want a connection with me. And if they want me, I have the upper hand. I can sell them a bottle of wine that costs as much as a coach seat on a commuter flight. I can get them to a private room and tell them NO TOUCHING. I can get gifts. I can sell them photos and panties and shoes and never ever let them do anything they really want to me.

This flies in the face of everything we are taught as women: be polite but not friendly. Dress in a feminine manner but don't reveal too much. Don't do anything to lead him on, because leading him on leads to assault.

And yeah, I was assaulted in the club. Private rooms are scary dark caves with pleather couches you go into with strange men while (hopefully) a bouncer stands a few yards away. I had to do an unbelievably acrobatic private dance once for a dude who was generally well behaved, but tried to touch my pussy every time it got within his hand's reach. I was pushed up against a wall by my throat by a guy who thought it would turn me on to dominate me. A dude stuck his nose between my ass cheeks while I was bent over in front of him. A bouncer (the one supposed to be protecting me) put his hand down my bra until I twisted his finger to get it out. He pressed the flat side of a cold champagne bottle against my ass when I was bent over in a private room, alone, to surprise me. "You owe me $100," I said.

He did not pay me $100.

I'm sure these experiences are mild compared to other dancers the world over. But the thing is, these experiences are mild compared to other women the world over. The assaults that I have endured from men as a civilian are much worse than those I endured in the club. And I never got paid for those. In the club, if someone is gross, you absolutely have the choice to walk away, to laugh in their face, to stop the dance - and keep the money. In the best case scenario, you even have giant, unsmiling men supporting your decision and walking you to the parking lot later.

In an office job, you have to decide every day not to correct sexist comments from Carl. Sure, you could become his personal teacher on feminism. But unlike a man at the club, Carl has unfettered access to you. You can't get away. So sometimes, many times, it is easier to just put up with it.

Because you're tired. Because you get catcalled on the street. Because the uber driver looks at you like a wolf looks at a lamb. Because you overhear a dude in the back of a bar say "I'm not attracted to fat chicks" or "women aren't funny" or "my ex-girlfriend is crazy" and you can't fix the whole world.

And when Carl moves you out of the way by touching your lower back or touches your arm too many times in a day, will you call human resources? Will you go through the "anonymous" sessions with the impartial contracted investigator? Will you stay at your job when Carl corners you outside of the building to angrily ask what the big deal is? When he starts torpedoing your relationship with the boss? When all of his friends do, too? Will you begin to dread everyday because of it?

Will your life be better or safer then?

I used to make certain I had enough energy to fight all of this. I corrected every stupid comment. I was the one who went to HR. I yelled at bros in bars. I was once the newest manager of a restaurant and my staff told me that the owner had been sexually harassing them and all his previous staffs for TWENTY YEARS. I warned the entire staff about him (with the permission of the ones under assault.) Upper management made my life hell. I quit. The rest of the staff went on strike, and not for higher pay. Simply to get the predator out of the building. I lived in fear for four months, unemployed, thinking he could "find me" or "get me."

And I have zero regrets. I truly felt like I may have had a chance to drag a prolific creep out into the daylight and protect his future victims. Perhaps if it was me being harassed, I would have put up with it, I can't say. Or I would have quit quietly and looked for a better situation, like many women do, in restaurants around the world. Stories of abuse in restaurants are so common as to become cliche.

That restaurant has a whole new staff now. They just reopened for brunch. The owner is just fine. I did the right thing, but what effect did it have on him? Not much. The effect on me was pure destruction.

Every woman, everywhere, has to put up with this shit. We are equally at risk for assault hanging off a pole with our tits out or wearing a turtleneck in a brightly lit office. We are at risk of making our lives harder if we complain. No one should be touched if they don't want it. But we are.

And whenever I can, I'm going to try and make money off of it.

Bartender

"True goodness is like water. Water's good for everything. It doesn't compete. It goes right to the low loathsome places, and so finds the way."

-Tao Te Ching by Lao Tzu (Translated by Ursula K. LeGuin)

—

While the server plays the role of the help, the bartender plays the role of slightly unattainable celebrity. The bartender is elevated above the servers. Servers are a dime a dozen, but there are only a few bartenders. Their sheer scarcity makes them an attractive creature. We started elevating bartenders further by calling them "mixologists." We liken bartending to a science and bartenders to experts in that science. It's laughable to imagine servers being rebranded as experts in "the science of waiting tables." Not because it is easier than bartending, or requires less skill, but because it is an important illusion that servers are your servants. If you dine on the floor, you want to feel a little bit better than someone else to feel better about yourself. You want all your tiniest whims to be fulfilled. You want to feel you are making decisions and the lowly server is executing them.

If you choose to dine at the bar, you don't need to be convinced to relinquish control and trust the bartender to guide the experience. You are fully aware that is what you are doing. If you dine at the bar, you want to get close to a mystery. Someone with skills and knowledge you don't have. You want a peek behind the curtain of how restaurants work. You feel better about yourself getting close to greatness, and your perception is that greatness rubs off on you.

You're different from other diners. You're better at going to restaurants. You feel magnanimous when the bartender is slammed and you don't get upset at the lack of attention. Not like those plebeians that dine on the floor, certainly! Huffing and puffing and flagging down their server with an undignified wave across the room. Beggars.

It is easier for you to feel safe relinquishing control at the bar because the bartender is always there. Servers can leave you adrift and scuttle off to disappear, unavailable for minutes at a time, off doing who knows what. My entire evening plays out directly in front of you. You can see exactly where all my effort is going. All my customers are right next to you for you to see the level of service I am offering. You try not to be jealous as I chat with that couple, as I laugh at that guy's joke, as I let that regular squeeze my hand affectionately. Any attention I bestow on you is a gift, not an expectation. You thrill when I finally flash a sparkling smile and stand directly in front of you to take your order calmly and patiently. (Especially because you can see how busy I am.) So you try to be quick, concise, and not co-opt my time. But boy, you'd love for me to come back.

That sense of being a resource with limited availability is deeply important in the club. When it was slow, I made sure to never just sit around and look at my phone where men could see me. I was always up, looking desirable. I chatted with the bartenders, flashed sultry smiles at regulars, made a round through the room using my most powerful sexy stroll on my own personal catwalk. If nothing happened, I would go to the dressing room for ten minutes and make a grand entrance back on the floor.

I'm not waiting for men. They're waiting for me.

There was a harmless regular, an old guy with an eastern European accent, and he would give you exactly one dollar each day IF he deigned to come up to the stage. I would usually say hello to him when we were slow. One day, a new man was sitting near the regular. Instead of going to the new guy, I went to the regular. We hugged, and chatted. I flirted. I gave him WAY more attention than I normally would. I subtly spread my legs and pulled my dress up high as I moved around in the chair. But all of this was angled at the new guy. Finally I departed the regular and made like I was going to walk away. At the last minute I tentatively moved towards the new guy and introduced myself.

I had that new guy in a private room in five minutes flat.

I had shown someone else was more worthy of my time. He got to see me shower attention on another man, and he wanted it for himself. When I finally shone the light of my attention on him, he was willing to pay to keep it.

It isn't as simple as "you're either a bar guy or a dining room guy." We aren't simply offering two different flavors of dream fulfillment. Even the guests on the floor are aware that the bartender is a thrilling attraction, a wealth of knowledge, a cut above the servers. "Ask your bartender if he can make a Diplomat," guests ask, not realizing an excellent server could probably answer the question. And as a server, we do promise to ask, because it is important to maintain the illusion that there is something elite and cool going on behind the bar.

When you think of a strip club, you think of the stage. You think of women doing amazing pole tricks and being showered in a deluge of cash. You think of men gathered around, fascinated and titillated by one talented woman.

Almost every stripper I know hates the stage. It's required for us to dance when they call our name. For us, it's our commercial to sell our wares. We get singles onstage, but we get hundreds slipped to us in private rooms.

I always liked the stage, even if it wasn't a big money maker. It feels thrilling to have all eyes on me. It feels cathartic to move my body to songs I like. It feels powerful to show off my naked body in a sexual way, to see the desire in men's eyes. Especially when the whole world says that lessens my power and my desirability.

I never even got good at the pole. My big trick was to step out of my long, flowy green dress, pole in one hand, dress in the other, and stroll around the pole with my dress flapping behind me like a military standard. Most of my dancing is considered "floor work." Writhing around on the stage, shoulder stands, swinging my hair, touching my body. All of these are elements that can be utilized in conjunction with the pole, but that is its own skill.

As the pandemic eased, I took a pole dancing class in a clean, well-lit studio. I paid a nice white lady for the privilege of learning an art form invented and perfected by black sex workers. While the practical skills are the same, I was astounded at the difference between dancing in a studio with other women compared to dancing on a stage for men. The studio is about artistry, confidence, and physical precision. The stage is about sex.

On stage, every move is anchored in mirroring sex. Every movement combination is a path back to spreading my legs for the audience. To running my fingers over my nipples. To slowly lifting my ass up and down as if I was sitting in a man's lap fucking him. To guiding men's eyes back to my barely covered pussy. It was there I felt powerful. In the studio, following choreography that mimicked sensuality without the need to embody it, I felt self-conscious, robotic, and embarrassed.

Pole dancing is a neat trick, an amazing skill, and can be useful in the club. However, many strippers I worked with were poor to fair at pole work. It made no impact on their profit. Ex-stripper turned crime scene technician Catherine Willows said on the show *CSI*, "The pole is there for a reason. It's what you hang on to so the creeps don't pull you out of there." I utterly disagree. The problem with the pole is that it is too far away from the men trying to put money in my underpants.

Nevertheless, the performative aspect of the stage at the center of the club or restaurant is important. Guests need a place to focus their awe, their appreciation, and their desire to be close to greatness. The sense of eliteness needs a physical heart in the building. A place for you to focus your awe.

Stripper costumes must be easy to take on and off. We do it twenty times a night. They must also be wrinkle-resistant since we're throwing them on the ground or over a chair. I usually wore a fancy bra, fancy thong, and a teeny tiny dress. I liked more material to play with, to create suspense to my nakedness. I wanted the men to start throwing money to encourage me to take my clothes off, not assume they'd reward me after the fact.

Bartenders are often required to wear similar uniforms to the waitstaff. But it is so important that I find a way to elevate my costume above the waitstaff. That may mean dressing more formally if the waitstaff dresses more casually. It may mean a dramatic cut of a dress that draws attention to how I move behind the bar. It may be a focus-pulling accessory like a bowtie or attention-grabbing earrings. If I'm going to be the star they put on stage all night, if I'm going to be cast as the elite artist, I need to dress the part.

As a bartender, you never leave the stage. Which is, honestly, a lot harder than just dancing for a set of three songs. What the bartender has that a stripper on stage does not is what Nick Miller from *New Girl* describes thus: "Look, these 18 inches of oak are the only thing that separates me from guys like Sid over there." Bartenders have the physical bar to protect them. But, there is an emotional toll that comes with always being visible to your guests. So, every bartender uses a valuable trick of body language called "the laugh away."

When you are saying something that feels like a natural point to do so, I'll point at you, or reach towards you and laugh. Leaving my arm extended to you for a moment, I'll quickly break eye contact, keep laughing, and start to walk away. Only then will I retract my arm. I don't have to wait for you to stop talking, and you don't feel ignored or abandoned.

What you really want when you sit at the bar is connection. You want community. You want to be recognized and welcomed. You hope for the possibility of a longer conversation, of friendship, and of acceptance.

The bartender might even lend you a sympathetic ear you desperately need. Because it isn't guaranteed, it doesn't feel transactional. We've all gone to bars and been ignored. And that feels terrible. You feel used. The transactional nature of the interaction is revealed and the magic is gone.

That's why the conclusion of the experience is just as important as the host's smiling greeting. Even if every service point has been hit, even if we had great rapport, if we don't actively make sure that the last thing you experience as you walk out the door is our appreciation, it has all been for naught.

In the club, after a dance, I always treated men like he had just given me an orgasm. I hug him on the floor for everyone to see how great he is and how much I like him. I act bashful and smitten. A make sure that he thinks this interaction was a big deal for me. If he isn't leaving the club right away, I make sure to go to the dressing room for a bit so that it feels like we just ended a date. If I were to walk off silently counting my money, I would reveal the transactional nature of our interaction. If we let you leave the bar without a heartfelt goodbye, no amount of empathetic listening over the course of the evening will register as sincere.

Being a rockstar bartender means you are more attached to us. It means you are more susceptible to be injured if we don't care for you tenderly. Being a rockstar isn't about being hot shit, it is about offering the highest level of intimate care.

Bar Manager

"Water and stone: what's softest in the world rushes and runs over what's hardest in the world. The immaterial enters the impenetrable"

-Tao Te Ching by Lao Tzu (Translated by Ursula K. LeGuin)

—

My club considered itself a "gentleman's club." Gentleman's clubs are billed as being classy, fancy, and just INCEDENTALLY happen to have naked ladies in them. We had to wear dresses (which we would eventually take off) and not just lingerie. There was a surprisingly great menu with steaks and lobster and salmon. The rooms for private parties were sleek and modern and anything that was in disrepair was impossible to see in the dark.

All our decisions as strippers stemmed from this vision of a higher-class strip club. We piggybacked on the vision the club had already created to bolster our own power. We didn't choose it, but we could manipulate it. We chose personas based on our looks and how that would work with the clientele that was attracted to this particular club. Our costumes were red and gold and black. Our names were Emily and Jennifer. We were Glamour Girl, Vixen, Crystal-studded Princess, Girl Next Door, Ingenue. I have long black hair and some prominent tattoos on my arms, so I always did better wearing black or red and projecting a bit of oversexed vixen than an innocent student trying to make rent.

The challenging part of honing a persona is that I saw a lot of men pass me by, and their money with them. I simply will not embody the perfect vision of sexual compatibility with everyone. But these are not lost sales. These men are paying money to a woman that tickles their fancy more than I do, and that's good for her. I simply cannot be all things to all men, and working my strengths helped me build a solid clientele who found them attractive.

As bar manager, I do not need to create a bar that is all things to all clients. I need to pick my identity and let every smaller decision be informed by that identity. There is a lot of alcohol in the world, and I don't need to sell all of it. There are a lot of trends in restaurants, and I don't need to surf all of them.

The biggest mistake bar managers make is menus that are way too long and complex. Now, long lists can have their place. If a bar's entire identity is having a bigger Spanish wine cellar than anyone in town, then that's a good reason to have a long list. If it's an Irish pub that can build marketing on having the biggest Irish whiskey selection in the tri-state area, that's a good reason. But having a long list, no matter how good a marketing angle it is, comes with problems. First of all: it is expensive. If guests come in and drink Woodford all the time but there is still an unopened bottle of Jefferson's Ocean on my shelf after three months, that's product the bar is paying to collect dust on the shelf, panache be damned.

Do I have space to store Jefferson's Ocean? Can the staff be educated to sell the Jefferson's Ocean? Do I have time to create an educational program? Is the staff invested in learning? Is the turnover so high that I educate them and they quit a month later?

I was the beverage director of a high end chain hotel with a fine dining restaurant and enormous bar. The company's flagship restaurant boasted a huge bourbon selection. In my city, we couldn't move 80% of the bourbon on the shelf. Every month I inventoried the same bottles, not a drop sold. It drove me mad. Finally, I moved most of it to the basement. With a smaller selection, I could more easily educate my staff. Once they sold through the lesser-known, unique bottles on the shelf, I would replace it with a different one from the basement and educate to that.

I was a bartender in a tiny French restaurant with a painfully long wine list. The bar could barely fit a bartender, let alone a refrigerator to chill fifty different white wines. They sat stacked in their dark cooler at floor level. When a guest ordered one, the only way to find it was for me to sit my ass directly on the linoleum and pull out every single bottle. Meanwhile, tickets for other tables piled up. It took so long to get that bottle to the table, I can't imagine a table was ever encouraged to order a bottle again. And god forbid they wanted a second bottle, because we probably only had one in stock.

Long lists are nothing but a dick swing. They are corvettes for a 55 year old middle manager with a tiny cock. If a bar manager can't find a place to stock the wine so their bartender can grab it easily, in a quantity enough they don't regularly run out, the only reason to insist on keeping that wine is pure penis envy.

It is important for you to think that bartenders and chefs are artists, creating wild and ethereal concoctions you can't get anywhere else. Mad geniuses. Mercurial creatives that need a long leash and complete freedom to achieve sublime culinary pleasures. But this isn't true.

While there is plenty of artistry and creativity in restaurants, most (almost all) of the job of the bartender is that of factory worker. We have to make it look like we are the most dazzling stripper in the joint, the one with the best pole tricks; money magnets as dollar bills shoot out of a plastic gun and stick to our naked skin under the spotlight for an adoring crowd. But all the while we are simply getting a ticket, making a round, and making it exactly the same as the day before. The bar manager supports this grind of factory work as best we can, with all the boring tasks required to do so.

In the club we keep our costumes simple so as to not confuse simple men, but we also keep them simple for consistency. If I dressed and acted like a sexed up vixen most days, and my regulars got used to that, and then suddenly I wore a frilly little princess dress, that's startling. There will be a subset of men that find it more attractive. Regulars I know well may even find it funny and charming. But consistency creates trust. Trust allows you to relinquish control. Relinquishing control allows us to guide your experience. And when you allow us to guide your experience, you have a better time.

Gregory Buda, the educational director for the Dead Rabbit ("The Best Bar in the World") says that, "Consistency is what builds trust in people who give you business. Because if they come in one night and have an amazing drink, and they come in the second night and it's – not even worse, but…different: you have just lost their trust in your entire establishment. Even if they don't know it, and even if you don't know it."

The fact is, guests don't want all the choices. You are tired of choosing. You know where you get every choice possible? The boring-ass grocery store.

Black beans. Seasoned black beans. No salt added black beans. Organic black beans.

Choice is banality. Choice is our own reflection in fluorescent light: pimpled, sagging, graying, and sad. What have you chosen with your infinite choice? The same old shit that made you into this.

You don't want everything. You want the one, perfect thing. You don't want all the girls, you want the girl that will finally reinforce your deepest hope that you're worthy, that you're special, just by being you.

You want a sparkling, charismatic rockstar to tell you, "you don't want that. You CAN'T have that. You want this. I want to initiate you into a better echelon of people, people who make better choices than you ever could.

"And all you need to do is: trust me."

There is nothing I HAVE to have on my menu. I don't have to have a cheap pinot grigio just because I think my customers expect it. I don't have to have ten wines available by the glass just because every other restaurant in town does. As long as I have a way to connect my choices clearly and purposefully to my bar's identity, any customers I lose will be customers I wouldn't want to keep.

Even if it is because I have poor storage. Even if it is because my sister was engaged to the president of an important wine distributor and their breakup was so rocky he won't touch my bar with a ten foot pole, I'm going to turn that into a specific narrative choice.

On Mad Men, when Lucky Strike fired the firm, Don Draper immediately turned around and wrote an open letter saying the firm has decided not to represent cigarettes due to ethical concerns. "And then, when Lucky Strike moved their business elsewhere, I realized, here was my chance to be someone who could sleep at night, because I know what I'm selling doesn't kill my customers." In reality, it was an enormous and unexpected loss, but he grabbed hold of the narrative to create a better narrative: I am fully in control. And the more I am in control, the more you trust me.

If I can only fit one draft keg, I make up a story as to why that one keg is the most delicious and hard to get keg in town. If I can only store 5 by-the-bottle wines, I write a story about how these wines are handpicked for specific, elite reasons. And if I must offer a product I'm not excited about because of demand, I make it the most expensive thing in the bar.

Sometimes, it is easier to offer a product that is familiar and sells easily. Sometimes, it is easier than educating my entire staff and every single guest that verdiccio is better than pinot grigio, and just fucking sell the pinot grigio. I quickly learned at my first bar managing gig that my patrons expected to have a cabernet by the glass. So I priced it 30% more than any other glass.

An illusion of exclusivity is only going to work if I can make money. I don't have standards, I have a story. I don't have preferences, I have a bottom line. I'll sell you what you want, but if you want it bad enough, I'll make you pay for it.

When I was at the club, the price of one lap dance was about as much as a purse from Target. The house took most of that. Maybe I'd get a tip, maybe not. Let me tell you: a lap dance is a lot of work. Maybe not dancing the length of a three minute song, sure. But building a relationship. The seduction. Gaining trust. Time unpaid before the dance. And, of course, entering an intimate space and taking my clothes off.

Lap dances are short, semi-private, and officially the customers can't touch you. Of course, they do. Private rooms pay more, but customer expectations are all over the place. Some men think they are going to get sex, some men want to touch you where you don't want to be touched. Girls do all kinds of things in private rooms– good for them. So, men expect what they had the last time, and that may not be something I'm comfortable doing. Lapdances are a challenge to make it seem like I can't wait to fuck a guy while barely touching him. I found it extremely fun.

My club had these big square armchairs in booths so I could climb up on the armrests and really utilize levels in space. Above him kneeling on the chair, at his level, or below him on the floor. I could do a handstand and land my feet behind the guy on the chair with my pussy in his face, and in an emergency, brace my feet against the chair while standing so he can't pull me into his lap. I move slowly, I stare deep into his eyes, I let him feel my breath against his neck. I take my dress off slowly, playfully. (This also buys me time to be a little further away from him.) I turn around and let him watch me unhook my bra, but I hold the cups on my breasts as I face him again. I wait as long as possible for the reveal, so that by the end of the three minutes, he is ready to get another dance.

I told men that I had a two dance minimum, and that a 20% tip would be paid up front. Did I lose sales with this tactic? Absolutely. But I made a lot more money in the long run with my limited time and energy. And I established myself as an elite product.

By far my weirdest customer in the club was a dude who told me he was waiting for another stripper. This is very common and not to be perceived as a hard "no." The other girl was actively ignoring this dude as hard as she could. He hemmed and hawed and wouldn't take me for a dance and was acting really weird. Finally, he pulled out a handwritten piece of paper and asked me to go read it in the locker room. And if I was up for his proposal, to come back out. He was so ashamed of what he wanted he couldn't look me in the eye. Turns out it was the most basic and boring babysitter fantasy. Truly, I probably could have given him a better time if he had just taken me for a regular dance. But he was consumed by this. He had brought an outfit to the club that he wanted a dancer to wear, tags still on it, in a Kohl's bag. That was also deeply boring: a plain white tank top, gym shorts, a scrunchie for my hair.

I said, "absofuckinglutely I'll do it."

He wanted to pay for one cheap lap dance in the costume, or to do it on the floor. I said, "oh, I'd love to! But if we do this, you'll be paying for me to change, the time for me to change, and role-playing. So we have to get an hour room." I stepped into the empty room next door to change and I took as much time as possible before I went over. And boy oh boy, was he gross and weird. It was not a fun time, he was not a cool guy, it was a grit-my-teeth-and-make-it-through-dance.

Did I feel demeaned? No. I felt twenty-eight Target purses richer. If I had let him waste all my time and do this specialized weird thing he wanted for cheap, I would have been letting him dictate the cost of my time. I could have walked away at any juncture if that wasn't the type of client I was willing to put up with. I came to this scenario in strength. He wanted it bad enough, so I made him pay for it.

And I dumped that Kohl's outfit in the trash on the way out the door, counting my money.

Conclusion

It took stripping to finally understand a lifetime in restaurants:

We are the fulfillers of dreams.

Restaurants and clubs are places where you can have your deepest desires and most wanton whims fulfilled by smiling, willing faces. In your day to day life, you're a mote. An irrelevant gray spot among ten million other irrelevant gray spots. Your wife is bored with you. Your boss wants to squeeze more work out of you. Your parents are disappointed in you. But here, in the spotlight of those smiling faces ready to serve, you can picture yourself as someone who matters. Someone whose opinions deserve to be heard. Someone who is sexy and charming and someone others look forward to seeing.

If you are in that heady elite where money can buy you anything, what do you long for? Where do you go? If you are a celebrity, where do you show off your magnetism and status?

Strip clubs. Restaurants.

The earthly value of money and the attraction to the unknowable intersect in the physical locations of strip clubs and restaurants. We are the altar that connects the divine and the terrestrial. We are the place everyone wants to be, even if they can afford everything. We are magic.

We're magic, but we are really not the fulfillers of dreams. We are the purveyors of the *illusion* that we are the fulfillers of dreams. We create a carefully crafted world where you think you can have anything you want.

But there are many limits. Last call is still at 1:45. The kitchen still closes at 10. There is no sex in the champagne room. Because we are just humans, of no greater or lesser worth than you, and we do not exist to serve. The fake eyelashes come off, the sweatpants come on, the pizza is delivered.

We're not cold-hearted. These are terribly taxing jobs physically, emotionally, and even to our personal safety. I've met plenty of people in both industries that are just in it for the money. But they don't last long. Of course there are real connections we form with our guests. Of course there are people we genuinely look forward to seeing. Chefs and bartenders care deeply about the creative process, standards of excellence, and pleasing their guests. Servers get a flush of pride when a table appreciates them. Strippers are proud of their skills on the pole and are moved when clients cry to us and tell us about heartbreak and disappointment. A connection purchased is still a connection had.

Restaurants and clubs are like little flowers poking through the cracks in an ocean of concrete. They are hope; hope this capitalist hellscape isn't the full story. Hope; that even though you are paying for a dance, maybe you will also luck into something authentic. It's our job to make you think you have.

But you're never getting all of us. You won't see our bad days unless we want you to. We work hard to make you think you are so special and we care so much about YOU SPECIFICALLY that's why we are going above and beyond. Feeling special is just the product you're paying for.

That may sound like a bummer. Especially, if right now you're recalling beautiful experiences you've had in restaurants or with sex workers, and could it be possible those were just lies? Just fictions? Just elaborate cons?

It's not a con, it's a service. Deep inside you there is a terrified question: am I worthy? Am I worthy of respect? Of attention? Of sexual connection? And I can tell you within the confines of raw honesty this book allows: I know you are.

We all are, and we've all been conned into thinking we are not. We've all been ground down by being cogs in someone else's machine. We are told rest is for the weak. We are told empathy is for the simple. We are all told we are lazy, and ugly, and unattractive, and vain, and even told we are dirty sluts with daddy issues.

To inhabit a world where we are worthy (a thing too vulnerable to even speak aloud), we must imagine it first. Everything ever created was imagined first. Any engineer or architect who had a flash of inspiration has grabbed a napkin and scribbled out their design. The design isn't real yet, and it never will be without that leap from imagination to blueprint. We help you make a blueprint of the you you want to be. In a restaurant, with a stripper, you get attention, respect, kindness, and stimulation. These are all things you deserve no matter what. We facilitate the invention of a you that has access to all of those things, a you that has yet to come. If you can't imagine that person first, you'll never become that person.

It's not just a moment. If it were just a moment you were buying, you wouldn't think of us as fulfillers of dreams. You'd just think of us as merchants with a service for sale. It's an entire creative space you're buying, with a chance to create a whole new life.

And that? That is beautiful.

Sources

Tzu, Lao. *Tao Te Ching*. Translated by Ursula K. LeGuin. Shambhala Press. 1997.

"Bathtub." *New Girl,* created by Elizabeth Meriwether, season 2, episode 10, Fox 2012

"Eleven Angry Jurors" *CSI,* created by Anthony E. Zuiker, season 4, episode 11. CBS 2003.

Keating, W. (Host). Buda, Gregory (Guest). (2021, April 12). The Science of Bartending (No. 1.1) [Audio podcast episode]. In *Business of Beverages*. businessofbeverages.com

"Blowing Smoke." *Mad Men*, created by Matthew Weiner, season 4, episode 12. Lionsgate Television, 2010.

About the Author

Peaches Kawamata has been working in the restaurant industry since 1996. In those decades, she has worked every role in front of house, and also as a dishwasher, expo and GM. Bar systems optimization and ergonomics are her main expertise, in which she helps bars better utilize poorly designed spaces, train staff, and unlock the creativity of their bartenders. She also used to dance around naked for money.

www.ingramcontent.com/pod-product-compliance
Lightning Source LLC
Chambersburg PA
CBHW060211260726

48658CB00005BA/1983